D1482906

ALL AROUND THE WORLD
EGYPT

by Jessica Dean

pogo

Ideas for Parents and Teachers

Pogo Books let children practice reading informational text while introducing them to nonfiction features such as headings, labels, sidebars, maps, and diagrams, as well as a table of contents, glossary, and index.

Carefully leveled text with a strong photo match offers early fluent readers the support they need to succeed.

Before Reading

- "Walk" through the book and point out the various nonfiction features. Ask the student what purpose each feature serves.
- Look at the glossary together. Read and discuss the words.

Read the Book

- Have the child read the book independently.
- Invite him or her to list questions that arise from reading.

After Reading

- Discuss the child's questions. Talk about how he or she might find answers to those questions.
- Prompt the child to think more. Ask: Pyramids were built to honor ancient pharaohs. How are leaders honored where you live?

Pogo Books are published by Jump!
5357 Penn Avenue South
Minneapolis, MN 55419
www.jumplibrary.com

Library of Congress Cataloging-in-Publication Data

Names: Dean, Jessica, 1963- author.
Title: Egypt / by Jessica Dean.
Other titles: All around the world.
Description: Minneapolis, MN : Jump!, Inc., 2018.
Series: All around the world
"Pogo Books are published by Jump!."
Ages 7-10. | Includes index.
Identifiers: LCCN 2017054178 (print)
LCCN 2017056995 (ebook)
ISBN 9781624969041 (hardcover ; alk. paper)
ISBN 9781624969058 (paperback)
ISBN 9781624969065 (e-book)
Subjects: LCSH: Egypt—Juvenile literature.
Classification: LCC DT49 .D336 2018 (print)
LCC DT49 (ebook) | DDC 962—dc23
LC record available at https://lccn.loc.gov/2017054178

Editor: Kristine Spanier
Book Designer: Molly Ballanger

Photo Credits: Photo Credits: Paul Hardy - Concept Stills and Motion/Getty, cover; Lotus_studio/Shutterstock, 1; Pixfiction/Shutterstock, 3; Dan Breckwoldt/Shutterstock, 4; Anton_Ivanov/Shutterstock, 5; N Mrtgh/Shutterstock, 6-7; bumihills/Shutterstock, 8-9; Suriya KK/Shutterstock, 9; Pius Lee/Shutterstock, 10; DEA/A. DAGLI ORTI/Getty, 11; Fotos593/Shutterstock, 12-13; Hang Dinh/Shutterstock, 14; Anadolu Agency/Getty, 15; Prin Adulyatham/Shutterstock, 16-17; Paul Cowan/Shutterstock, 18-19; B.O'Kane/Alamy, 20-21; kivandam/Shutterstock, 23.

Printed in the United States of America at Corporate Graphics in North Mankato, Minnesota.

TABLE OF CONTENTS

CHAPTER 1

WELCOME TO EGYPT!

pyramid

Would you like to gaze at the Great Sphinx? Or visit ancient **pyramids**?

Do you want to ride on a camel? Or take a trip down the Nile River? Egypt is a country full of adventure!

The Sahara **Desert** is here. Sand stretches as far as the eye can see. Sand foxes, snakes, and gazelles live in the desert.

Water springs up in surprising places. Cities and farms spread out nearby. Around them are miles and miles of desert.

WHAT DO YOU THINK?

A desert area with water is called an **oasis**. Why do you think cities and farms are found near these?

Sahara
Desert

Nile River

The Nile River flows through Egypt. It is the longest river in the world. The **papyrus** plant grows on the banks of the Nile. **Ancient** Egyptians used it to make paper.

DID YOU KNOW?

Nile crocodiles are long, too. In fact, they can grow up to 10 feet (3 meters) long!

papyrus · · · ▶

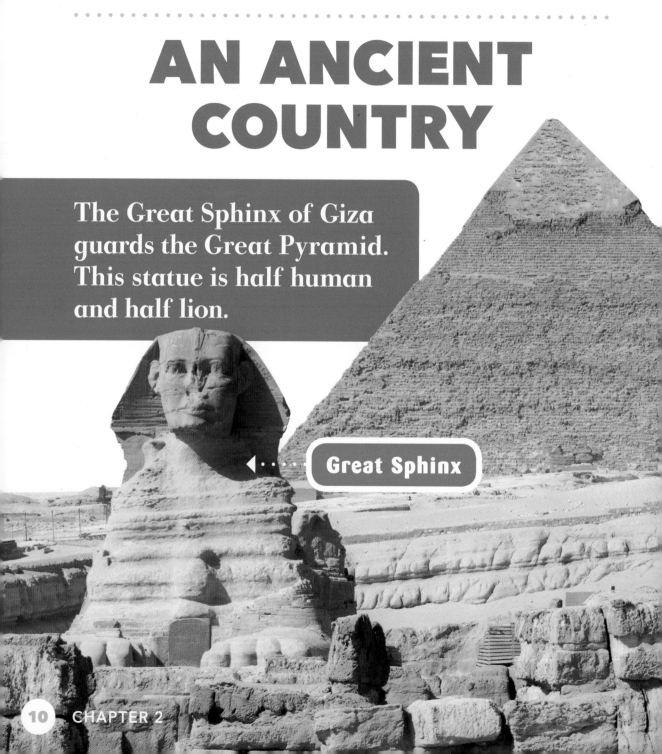

CHAPTER 2

AN ANCIENT COUNTRY

The Great Sphinx of Giza guards the Great Pyramid. This statue is half human and half lion.

Great Sphinx

The pyramids were built more than 4,500 years ago. **Pharaohs** were buried inside. They were the first kings of Egypt. Their **burial chambers** were filled with riches.

burial chamber

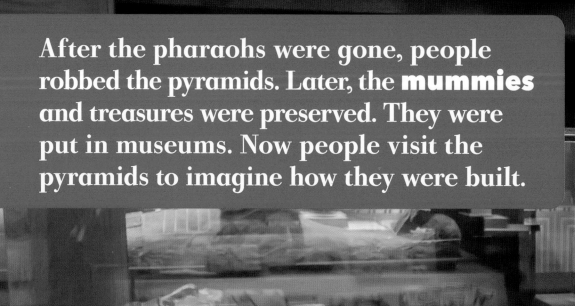

After the pharaohs were gone, people robbed the pyramids. Later, the **mummies** and treasures were preserved. They were put in museums. Now people visit the pyramids to imagine how they were built.

TAKE A LOOK!

The Great Pyramid has different rooms inside.
Each room once had a special purpose.

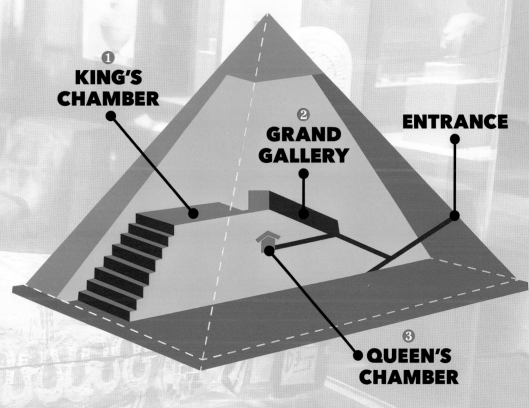

① **KING'S CHAMBER**
② **GRAND GALLERY**
ENTRANCE
③ **QUEEN'S CHAMBER**

① **King's Chamber: burial chamber of the pharaoh Khufu**
② **Grand Gallery: leads to the king's chamber;**
   ceiling is almost 30 feet (9 m) high
③ **Queen's Chamber: may have held special objects but**
   was not meant to be the burial chamber for the queen

CHAPTER 3
LIFE IN EGYPT

In the country, homes are built with mud bricks. Some are painted bright, cheerful colors. Most have only a few rooms.

Farmers grow **crops** in the Nile Valley. Egypt **exports** fruit and vegetables to other countries.

The big cities here are very crowded. Tall buildings line narrow streets. Tiny apartments are inside.

Cairo is the **capital**. It has more people than places to live. Many city workers have **service jobs**. They work in stores, banks, and schools.

DID YOU KNOW?

The people of Egypt vote for the president. Then the president chooses a **prime minister**.

VOTE

Cairo

Nile River

flatbread · · · · ▶

Food here is fresh and simple. Fruit with yogurt or cheese is breakfast or a snack. Many meals offer beans, vegetables, and rice. Meat is not served often. Flatbread comes with every meal.

Sweets are simple, too. Fruit and nuts are sweetened with honey. They are served on ice cream or cake. Rice pudding is another favorite treat.

WHAT DO YOU THINK?

Kids here eat nuts and fresh grapes. They eat cucumbers or peppers with dips. Are these different from or similar to snacks you eat?

Egyptians greet spring with Sham el-Nessim. It is a day for picnics and outdoor fun. Ramadan is celebrated here, too. People don't eat or drink during the day. They light lanterns to celebrate. Friends gather for a special meal after the sun goes down.

There is a lot to experience in Egypt. What would you like to do here?

lanterns

QUICK FACTS & TOOLS

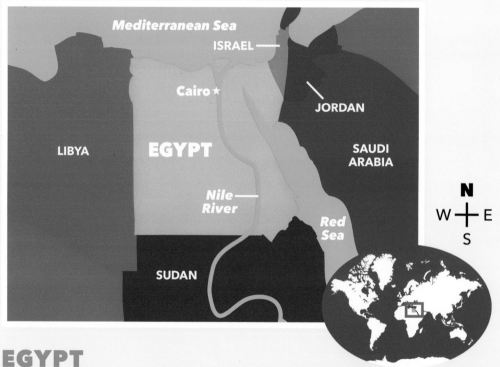

EGYPT

Location: Africa

Size: 386,662 square miles (1 million square kilometers)

Population: 97,041,072 (July 2017 estimate)

Capital: Cairo

Type of Government: presidential republic

Language: Arabic

Exports: oil, gas, fruits, vegetables, cotton, textiles, metal products

GLOSSARY

ancient: Very old.

burial chambers: Rooms used to bury the remains of the dead.

capital: A city where government leaders meet.

crops: Plants grown for food.

desert: A dry area where hardly any plants grow because there is so little rain.

exports: Sells goods to other countries.

mummies: Dead bodies that have been preserved with special chemicals and wrapped in cloth.

oasis: A place in a desert where water can be found above the ground and where plants and trees can grow.

papyrus: A tall water plant that grows in northern Africa and southern Europe and from which paper can be made.

pharaohs: Kings in ancient Egypt.

prime minister: The leader of a country.

pyramids: Ancient Egyptian stone monuments where pharaohs and their treasures were buried.

service jobs: Jobs and work that provide services for others, such as hotel, restaurant, and retail positions.

INDEX

TO LEARN MORE

Learning more is as easy as 1, 2, 3.

1) Go to www.factsurfer.com

2) Enter "Egypt" into the search box.

3) Click the "Surf" button to see a list of websites.

With factsurfer, finding more information is just a click away.